INSPIRATIONAL
POEMS
from the
HEART.

Inspirational Poems *from the* Heart.

Bobby Russell

XULON PRESS

Xulon Press
2301 Lucien Way #415
Maitland, FL 32751
407.339.4217
www.xulonpress.com

© 2021 by Bobby Russell

All rights reserved solely by the author. The author guarantees all contents are original and do not infringe upon the legal rights of any other person or work. No part of this book may be reproduced in any form without the permission of the author.

Due to the changing nature of the Internet, if there are any web addresses, links, or URLs included in this manuscript, these may have been altered and may no longer be accessible. The views and opinions shared in this book belong solely to the author and do not necessarily reflect those of the publisher. The publisher therefore disclaims responsibility for the views or opinions expressed within the work.

Unless otherwise indicated, Scripture quotations taken from the New American Standard Bible (NASB). Copyright © 1960, 1962, 1963, 1968, 1971, 1972, 1973, 1975, 1977, 1995 by The Lockman Foundation. Used by permission. All rights reserved.

Paperback ISBN-13: 978-1-66283-427-1
Hard Cover ISBN-13: 978-1-66283-997-9
Ebook ISBN-13: 978-1-66283-428-8

"A Prayer"

A prayer can help when you are sad,
A prayer can help make you glad,
A prayer can keep you from sin,
Only if you accept Christ as savior and friend.
A prayer is handy any old time,
It is also handy when you are trying to rhyme.
A prayer is best when on your knees,

God even likes to hear a please.
I love to pray on my knees in the day,
So please get on your knees and see what he will say,
A prayer will help you speak to him,
A prayer could help you through his realm.
A prayer can reach out to God our friend,
Turn Satan away, and let God come in,
A prayer tells us what we must know.
For God loves us and helps us grow.
Don't you want Christ in your life?
Cause Satan will stab you like a knife.
So put "A Prayer" in your heart and soul.
And send Satan back to that Deep Dark Hole.

Bobby Russell

"Heaven Will Open"

When Satan comes up to make his heist,
We the people will call on our Christ.
He will come down and keep us from harm,
And take us to heaven in his loving arms.
The angels will come and sing to us,
Then we will see Jesus, for He is a must.
Our Lord Jesus wants us to do right,
He wants us to love and not to fight.
Then Heaven will open this we know,
Our love for everyone will then surely grow.
Yes, Heaven will open and we will be cared for,
God of Christ will meet us at the door.
God will stomp Satan through the sand,
God can beat Satan with just one hand.
The scriptures then will all be filled,
Satan will finally then be killed.

Bobby Russell

"God's Creations"

God has made the animals and trees,
He has also made the birds and bees,
He has created a lot of things,
He has made insects that really stings.
He's created the sky and the clouds above,
He has helped me and and woman to fall in love,
He created all the ocean floors,
He has even opened a lot of doors.
He gave man and woman knowledge to know,
Just how to keep us and help us grow.
He does not mind if we are black or white,
As long as we help each other and do not fight.
He will help us one and all,
He will even help an infant to crawl.
Now we know of God's Creation,
I believe he will help our corrupt nation.
He surely knows of drugs and punks,
He even knows of our city's drunks.
He will clear it up in him own time,
He will even clean up the Nation's crime

Bobby Russell

"Dear God You are the One"

Where does the sun come from,
Where does the moon get it's light,
When do the stars come out,
Is it Satan dwelling in the night.
Does the world get to much of sin,
Will the good guys for Jesus ever win.
All the bad guys carrying guns around,
When will all this crime slow down.
"Dear God", you're the one that will defeat,
You are the All Mighty to put sin to sleep,
"Dear God" I call on you to help me out,
This battle with Satan, has got my doubts.
There is a fear inside my soul,
I feel I'm slipping inside his evil hole.
The darkness is falling down on me.
It is that evil man it just has to be.
"Dear God" you're the one that will defeat,
You're the All Mighty to put sin to sleep.
"Dear God" I call on you to help me out,
This battle with Satan has got my doubts.

Bobby Russell

"Oh Jesus I Need You"

Dear Jesus my heart is in your hands,
I need you to please understand.
I'll swallow all my pride,
I need you to be my guide.
Oh Jesus I love you and need you so,
Dear Jesus, How I long for my need to grow.
Oh how I really care,
When I need you, you're always there.
Please open up your heart,
And let in a brand new start,
I'll do whatever you say,
If you will just love me every single day.
I'd lay my life on the line for you,
Cause when I get to heaven I'll be new.
If all the people, they only could see,
What the world would be like without you and me.
Dear Jesus, I love, I need, I want you here,
Please stay with me, I feel you near.
Oh Jesus, I need you close by me,
Destroy Satan so he will never be.

Bobby Russell

"The Son of God"

He's the soul of our salvation,
He can save us while on vacation,
He's the man with the plan,
His power is love and also grand.
He is the way, the truth, and life,
He can save you from so much strife.
Except a man be born again,
If he goes to heaven, he will not sin.
For as in Adam all will die,
Even so, in Christ shall all be alive.
The wages of sin is sorrowful death,
And with that, we will take our last breath.
The Son of God is the only one to fear,
When He comes down, his trumpets we will hear.
Salvation is brought on by a spiritual birth,
That getting to see Jesus is what it's worth.
The wicked then shall be turned into Hell,
Down, Down, falling in a bottomless well.
So let the Son of God be our Father,
And Satan never again will be a bother.

Bobby Russell

"Getting Saved"

Jesus is here to get you Saved,
So don't sit around and rant and rave.
You've got no excuse not to repent,
Jesus is coming from God, he was sent.
Look up people, see what it is about.
If you are lost then getting saved is the route.
When you don't know Jesus, this is bad,
Call on Jesus, and make Satan really mad.
Getting saved is the right thing to do,
Getting Saved is really being true.
If you have doubt in your Salavation,
Jesus is your closest relation.
When you have done really wrong,
Getting Saved can make you strong,
Jesus will be there, just wait and see,
I know! Caused He really helped me.

Bobby Russell

"Ask for Jesus"

If you have a problem and can't solve it,
Get on your knees and look up, and pray a little bit.
Just ask for Jesus, he is the answer.
You can't get any more fancier.
If you feel down and cant get going,
Ask for Jesus, and He'll keep you growing.
If you ever in doubt, and feel blue,
Ask for Jesus, then you will feel brand new.
When things are tough and really bad,
Ask for Jesus, in prayer you will be glad.
When Satan tells you to do so wrong,
Ask for Jesus, it is he who really belongs.
If you find a scripture you don't understand,
Ask for Jesus, He's your man.
When you feel confused and really abused,
Ask for Jesus, for He'll never refuse.
If you haven't been saved, and really want to,
Ask for Jesus, he has a Glorious Crew.
When you feel temptation coming on,
Ask for Jesus and it won't last long.

Bobby Russell

"A Prayer for All"

The gospel of prayer is so sweet,
The word of God cannot be beat.
Jesus is the Son of God, and was anointed,
To have all the power he was appointed.
True prayer is a two way communication,
That through God, makes our creations,
Who may ascent into the hill of the Lord,
Whoever we are, we will not be bored.
He who has a prayer in pure heart,
With Jesus it's a wonderful start,
And the Lord, who you seek,
Will come to you when you are weak.
Prayer changes people, and they change things,
The Glory of Power is what it brings,
My love and my strength I get through Prayer,
I call on Jesus Christ he is always there.

Bobby Russell

"The Four of Us"

I love the country life it's so great,
It is Satan's name I really hate.
In Jesus name I want to learn,
When I am in heaven, I know I've earned.
The four of us will be so proud,
We will shout it so very loud.
My Mom and Dad and Me,
We will serve and Jesus will be glad.
The Lord has taught, and given me,
The wisdom to know it was meant to be.
The four of us, that I speak of,
Will dwell in heaven from above.
When he comes and dressed in white,
Then we will know to stop the fight,
We will be warriors for Jesus Christ,
And then Satan cannot make his heist
The four of us, we will then depart,
So in the end, we will play it smart.
We will have been saved, and sent nod.

Bobby Russell

"Corruption of Sin"

Why do the nations conspire,
Why does Hell have the fire.
God has his reasons and they are real,
With Satan, he does not deal.
To the Lord I cry aloud,
And he answers from a holy cloud.
My dear son, in my own time,
I will clean up the world's crime.
Dear Lord, I praise you with all my heart,
This world is so evil soon it will fall apart.
All the violence and crime will halt,
Satan then will be at fault.
Brother against brother, nation against nation,
That will be the results, without salvation.
Corruption of sin is where its starts,
If you are not saved, with Jesus you will not part.

Bobby Russell

"I have Praised Him"

I have praised His for is love is true,
He makes me happy, when I am blue,
I have praised Him, and still doing so,
When I pray it helps me grow.
I have praised Him when I was sad,
And still doing so,
When I pray it helps me grow.
I have praised His, at my best,
I go into prayer, then I rest.
I have praised him for awhile,
When I look up, I feel his smile.
I have praised him in the day,
When I do to go Heaven I know I'll stay.
I have praised Him, and his glory,
Now I'll not have any worry,
I have praised Him this is true,
Maybe he will come for me and you.

Bobby Russell

"My Love For God"

When I do anything wrong,
With God it doesn't last long.
When I say something bad,
God lets me know he is sad.
Show me your path of Lord,
With your word I'm never bored.
To you Dear God, I lift up my soul.
Out of darkness that's black as coal.
Remember not the sins of my youth,
Stay with me Lord, and I will tell the truth.
Hear my voice when I call,
Shine your light so I will not fall.
I will love your house where your glory dwells,
I will love the sound of your Heavenly bells.
I will love the light that shines so Great,
I wanna be with you in your beautiful estate.
My love for you Lord, is so true,
That just your presence makes me new.
Whatever sins that are in my past,
My dear Lord will rid them fast.

Bobby Russell

CPSIA information can be obtained
at www.ICGtesting.com
Printed in the USA
LVHW012116231221
707002LV00004B/50